THE NEW AMERICA
NEWSOM CONTROVERSIES & HIDDEN AGENDAS

BY JON ROBERT QUINN

The Risks of Ambition

As the national profile of Gavin Newsom continued to grow, so did the conversation around what his leadership represents—not just for California, but for the country as a whole. Ambition in leadership is often necessary. It drives change, pushes boundaries, and challenges outdated systems. But ambition also brings with it a level of scrutiny that few are fully prepared for, especially when the outcomes of policy decisions affect millions of people in real time.

California has long been viewed as a proving ground for bold ideas. It is a state that leads culturally, economically, and politically. From technology to entertainment to environmental policy, what happens in California often sets the tone for the rest of the nation. That influence naturally places its leadership under a microscope. In many ways, California is not just a state—it is a preview of what could come next.

Under Newsom's leadership, the state has embraced a series of forward-looking policies designed to address long-standing issues such as income inequality, worker protections, and access to opportunity. One of the most widely discussed examples has been the move to raise the minimum wage for fast food workers to $20 per hour. Supporters see this as a meaningful step toward improving quality of life for workers who have historically operated on the margins of the economy. For many families, even a modest increase in wages can translate into greater stability, better access to housing, and an improved sense of dignity in their work.

At the same time, policies of this scale rarely operate in isolation. Economic systems are interconnected, and even well-intentioned changes can produce ripple effects that require careful navigation. For business owners—particularly small and mid-sized operators—higher labor costs can introduce new challenges. Some respond by adjusting pricing, others by streamlining operations, and some by reevaluating long-term sustainability. These are not signs of failure, but rather indicators of an evolving economic environment.

The restaurant industry, which plays a significant role in California's economy, offers a clear example of this balancing act. On one hand, higher wages can lead to a more stable and motivated workforce. On the other, businesses must adapt to maintain profitability in an increasingly competitive landscape. This dynamic creates a tension that is not easily resolved, but it is also where innovation tends to emerge. New business models, automation strategies, and operational efficiencies often develop in response to these pressures.

What becomes clear is that progress is rarely linear. Efforts to raise standards in one area can create new considerations in another. This does not invalidate the intent behind the policy—it simply underscores the complexity of governing a large and diverse economy. California's experience highlights an important reality: meaningful change requires both vision and adaptability.

Another dimension of this conversation centers on the broader cost of living. As wages increase, there is often a corresponding shift in pricing across goods and services. This phenomenon is not unique to California, but it is more visible in a state where the cost of living is already among the highest in the nation. The challenge, then, is not just about raising wages, but about ensuring that those increases translate into real, lasting improvements in quality of life.

These are the kinds of issues that naturally follow a leader onto the national stage. As speculation has grown around Newsom's future—including his potential role in future presidential elections—California becomes a case study in both opportunity and complexity. Voters across the country are not just looking at policies in theory; they are looking at outcomes in practice.

Newsom's public support for Joe Biden has positioned him as a loyal and strategic figure within the Democratic Party. At the same time, his visibility has increased through national media appearances, policy advocacy, and international engagement. His visit to China and meeting with Xi Jinping, for example, drew attention not only for its diplomatic significance but also for what it signaled about his role on the global stage.

International engagement is a natural extension of leadership in a state like California, which operates as one of the largest economies in the world. Building relationships, discussing climate initiatives, and participating in global dialogue are all part of that responsibility. At the same time, these moments contribute to a broader narrative about readiness for national leadership. They reflect a leader who is thinking beyond state lines, while also inviting discussion about how those experiences translate into federal governance.

Within political circles, conversations about the future are constant. Whether tied to election cycles or shifts in leadership, there is always an undercurrent of "what's next." In Newsom's case, that conversation includes questions about timing, positioning, and the broader direction of the Democratic Party. He represents a certain energy—articulate, media-savvy, and willing to engage in high-stakes debates. For some, that is exactly what the party needs. For others, it raises questions about how bold policy ideas perform when scaled nationally.

It is important to recognize that every leadership approach comes with trade-offs. Policies designed to address systemic inequality may require adjustments in other areas of the economy. Efforts to protect workers may require businesses to rethink traditional models. These are not flaws—they are realities of governing in a complex system.

Supporters of Newsom often point to his willingness to act decisively. In an era where many leaders are criticized for inaction, there is value in taking a clear stance and moving forward. His policies reflect a belief that government can play an active role in shaping a more equitable society. That perspective resonates with many who feel that incremental change is no longer sufficient.

At the same time, thoughtful leadership also involves evaluating outcomes and making adjustments where necessary. The most effective leaders are not those who avoid challenges, but those who respond to them with clarity and flexibility. California's ongoing evolution provides a real-time example of how policy decisions unfold over time, offering insights that extend far beyond state borders.

For voters, the question is not simply whether a leader has ambition—it is how that ambition is applied. Does it lead to sustainable progress? Does it account for the full spectrum of economic realities? Does it create opportunities not just in theory, but in practice?

These are not easy questions, and they do not have simple answers. What California demonstrates is that leadership at this level is as much about managing complexity as it is about setting direction. It requires a willingness to engage with competing priorities, to listen to diverse perspectives, and to make decisions in an environment where perfect outcomes are rarely possible.

In many ways, the conversation around Newsom reflects a broader national dialogue about the future of leadership. What kind of policies will define the next decade? How do we balance innovation with stability? How do we create systems that work for both workers and businesses in a rapidly changing world?

These are the stakes that come with ambition. They are not unique to any one individual, but they become more visible when a leader operates at a high level of influence. California, with all of its strengths and challenges, offers a lens through which these questions can be explored.

Through platforms like *The Jon Robert Quinn Podcast*, these conversations continue to reach audiences who are looking for more than surface-level analysis. They are looking for context, perspective, and a deeper understanding of how policy decisions impact everyday life. That is where real value is created—not in taking sides, but in examining the full picture.

As the country continues to evolve, leaders like Newsom will remain part of the national conversation. His approach, his policies, and his trajectory will be analyzed, debated, and interpreted from multiple angles. That is the nature of public leadership at this level.

In the end, ambition is neither inherently positive nor negative. It is a force. What matters is how that force is directed, how it adapts, and how it ultimately serves the people it is meant to represent. California's experience does not provide all the answers, but it does offer something equally valuable—a real-world perspective on what it takes to lead in a time of constant change.

And for a nation watching closely, that perspective may prove to be one of the most important factors in shaping what comes next.

A Leadership Under Pressure

The tenure of Gavin Newsom as Governor of California has been defined by visibility, urgency, and a willingness to take on complex issues head-on. In a state as large and influential as California, leadership is never quiet. Every decision carries weight, every policy invites reaction, and every moment is subject to public interpretation. With that level of exposure comes pressure—not just to lead, but to lead in a way that resonates across a wide and often divided population.

California is not an easy state to govern. It operates as one of the largest economies in the world, with a population more diverse than most countries. The expectations placed on its leadership are immense, and the margin for error is small. Against that backdrop, Newsom's time in office has included a mix of ambitious reforms, strong advocacy, and moments that sparked intense public conversation.

One of the most defining moments of his governorship came in 2021, when a recall election placed his leadership directly in the hands of voters. Recall efforts are not uncommon in California politics, but qualifying for the ballot requires a significant level of organization and public engagement. The fact that the recall moved forward demonstrated that there was a meaningful segment of the population seeking a different direction. At the same time, the outcome of that election reaffirmed that a majority of voters supported Newsom's continued leadership, highlighting the complexity of public opinion in a state as multifaceted as California.

In the years since, discussions around accountability, performance, and direction have remained part of the broader political conversation. Advocacy groups and community leaders have continued to raise concerns about issues such as affordability, public safety, education, and the overall cost of living. These concerns are not unique to one administration—they reflect long-standing challenges that have evolved over decades. What changes is how each leader chooses to address them.

From Newsom's perspective, many of his policy decisions have been rooted in a desire to expand access and create more equitable outcomes. Initiatives related to healthcare access, criminal justice reform, and social services have been positioned as efforts to modernize systems that many believe were overdue for change. Supporters see these moves as necessary steps toward a more inclusive and forward-thinking California.

At the same time, policy shifts of this scale often generate debate about implementation and outcomes. Expanding services requires funding. Reforming systems requires time. And in a state where expectations are high, progress is often measured not just by intent, but by visible results. This creates an environment where every policy is evaluated from multiple angles—economic, social, and practical.

Public discourse around taxation, business climate, and government spending has remained active throughout Newsom's tenure. California's position as a hub for innovation and entrepreneurship brings both opportunity and pressure. Business owners, workers, and policymakers all have a stake in how the state evolves. For some, the focus is on maintaining competitiveness and encouraging growth. For others, the priority is ensuring that growth translates into broader access and opportunity.

These conversations are part of a larger balancing act —one that exists in every major economy. How do you support business development while also protecting workers? How do you invest in social programs while maintaining fiscal stability? These are not simple questions, and they do not have one-size-fits-all answers. What California demonstrates is that leadership requires navigating these tensions in real time, often under intense public scrutiny.

Another defining chapter of Newsom's governorship was the COVID-19 pandemic, a period that tested leaders across the globe. Decisions had to be made quickly, often with limited information and evolving guidance. In California, policies around business closures, public health measures, and school operations became central to the state's response.

Looking back, it is clear that the pandemic created challenges that extended far beyond public health. Economic disruption, shifts in education, and changes in daily life affected nearly every household. As more data and analysis have emerged over time, there has been ongoing discussion about what worked, what could have been handled differently, and how to better prepare for future crises. These conversations are not about assigning blame—they are about learning and adapting in an environment where the stakes were extraordinarily high.

One moment that drew significant public attention during that period was Newsom's attendance at a dinner at The French Laundry. The event became a widely discussed example of the challenges leaders face in aligning personal actions with public expectations. To his credit, Newsom acknowledged the situation and stated that he should have exercised better judgment. In leadership, moments like these can become defining—not because they represent the entirety of a record, but because they shape public perception in a very immediate way.

Beyond state-level governance, Newsom has also taken on a more visible national role. His public support for Joe Bidenand Kamala Harris has positioned him as an active participant in the broader direction of the Democratic Party. He has engaged in national debates, participated in campaign efforts, and used media platforms to advocate for policy positions he believes in.

This increased visibility naturally leads to questions about the future. Conversations around potential presidential ambitions are not unusual for a leader operating at this level. In many ways, it is part of the progression of modern politics. Leaders who demonstrate the ability to manage complex systems and communicate effectively often find themselves considered for roles beyond their current position.

At the same time, moving from state leadership to national leadership introduces a new level of scale. Policies that are implemented in one state must be evaluated in the context of an entire country, with its own regional differences, economic structures, and political dynamics. What works in California may require adjustment elsewhere. That does not diminish the value of those policies—it simply reinforces the importance of adaptability.

Newsom's engagement on the national stage, including high-profile discussions and interactions with leaders across the political spectrum, reflects a broader effort to shape conversations beyond California. His debate with Ron DeSantis, for example, highlighted contrasting approaches to governance and policy. These moments are not just political theater—they are opportunities for voters to see how leaders articulate their vision under pressure.

As with any public figure, perspectives on Newsom vary. Supporters point to his willingness to take action, his communication skills, and his focus on addressing systemic challenges. They see a leader who is not afraid to engage with difficult issues and who believes in using government as a tool for progress.

Others take a more cautious view, emphasizing the importance of measuring long-term outcomes and ensuring that policies achieve their intended goals. They highlight the need for balance—between ambition and execution, between innovation and stability.

Both perspectives contribute to a more complete understanding of leadership. In reality, effective governance often requires elements of both—vision to set direction and discipline to ensure that direction translates into results.

As California continues to evolve, it remains a powerful example of what it means to govern in a complex, high-stakes environment. The state's challenges—housing, affordability, economic inequality—are not isolated issues. They are part of a broader national conversation about how to build systems that work in a rapidly changing world.

For Newsom, the path forward will likely continue to involve navigating these dynamics while maintaining a clear sense of direction. Leadership at this level is not about avoiding criticism—it is about engaging with it, learning from it, and using it as a tool for refinement.

For the country, the conversation extends beyond any one individual. It is about understanding the qualities that define effective leadership in the years ahead. It is about recognizing that progress often comes with complexity, and that meaningful change requires both courage and careful execution.

In that sense, California serves as more than just a backdrop—it serves as a real-time case study. The decisions made, the outcomes achieved, and the lessons learned all contribute to a larger narrative about where the country is headed.

And as that narrative continues to unfold, one thing remains clear: leadership under pressure reveals not just the challenges of the moment, but the potential for what comes next.

The High Cost of High Wages

In cities like Los Angeles, where opportunity and pressure coexist on nearly every corner, economic policy is never abstract—it's personal. It shows up in rent payments, grocery bills, hiring decisions, and the daily reality of work. So when Gavin Newsom signed legislation raising the minimum wage for fast food workers to $20 per hour, it was more than a headline. It was a moment that captured the ongoing evolution of California's economic identity.

At its core, the policy was rooted in a straightforward idea: workers who contribute to the economy should be able to sustain a reasonable quality of life. For many fast food employees, this increase represented more than just a higher hourly rate—it offered the possibility of greater financial stability, reduced reliance on assistance programs, and a stronger sense of economic participation. In a state where the cost of living continues to rise, even incremental improvements can have meaningful impact.

The announcement itself reflected that sense of progress. Workers, advocates, and labor leaders saw it as the result of years of organizing and persistence. Behind the scenes, it represented the culmination of extensive negotiations between labor groups, business interests, and policymakers. Agreements of this scale rarely happen overnight. They are built through compromise, recalibration, and a recognition that multiple perspectives must be accounted for.

Newsom framed the decision as an acknowledgment of the modern workforce. He pushed back on the long-standing perception that fast food jobs are primarily held by teenagers or temporary workers, instead emphasizing that many of these roles are filled by adults supporting families and building long-term stability. In that context, the wage increase was positioned not just as an economic adjustment, but as a recognition of contribution.

Stories from workers helped bring that perspective into focus. Individuals balancing multiple responsibilities—raising families, managing expenses, and maintaining consistent employment—stood as real-world examples of why the conversation around wages continues to evolve. For them, the policy was not theoretical. It was immediate.

At the same time, policies of this magnitude naturally introduce broader economic considerations. Wage increases do not exist in isolation; they interact with pricing structures, operational costs, and long-term business planning. For restaurant operators, particularly franchise owners working within tight margins, higher wages require strategic adjustments. Some may look to increase efficiency, others may reevaluate pricing, and some may explore new models altogether.

This is where the conversation becomes more nuanced. Economic systems are interconnected, and shifts in one area often create movement in another. As wages rise, businesses respond in ways that allow them to remain viable. That response can take many forms—menu pricing adjustments, changes in staffing models, or investments in technology designed to streamline operations. None of these outcomes are inherently negative; they are part of how markets adapt.

The restaurant industry, in particular, has always been highly responsive to change. It is an industry built on thin margins, high competition, and constant reinvention. The introduction of a higher wage floor accelerates that process. For some establishments, it creates pressure. For others, it creates opportunity— to rethink how they operate and to differentiate themselves in a changing market.

One of the more innovative elements of the legislation was the creation of a Fast Food Council, designed to provide ongoing oversight and adjustments to wage standards through 2029. By tying potential increases to inflation, the policy attempts to create a more dynamic system—one that evolves with economic conditions rather than remaining fixed. This reflects a broader shift toward adaptive policymaking, where long-term sustainability is part of the design.

Still, the relationship between wages and cost of living remains a central consideration. As income levels rise, there can be corresponding shifts in the price of goods and services. This is not unique to California—it is a common feature of economic systems—but it becomes more visible in high-cost regions. The challenge is ensuring that wage growth translates into real purchasing power, rather than being offset by rising expenses.

This dynamic often leads to what economists describe as a "reset" effect, where increases in wages gradually align with increases in costs. The goal, then, is not simply to raise wages, but to create conditions where those wages deliver lasting value. That requires ongoing attention to housing, supply chains, taxation, and overall economic balance.

Another important dimension of this policy is the role of negotiation. The agreement that led to the wage increase involved trade-offs on multiple sides. Labor groups adjusted certain priorities, while business organizations reconsidered others. This kind of compromise is often where meaningful progress happens—not in absolute wins or losses, but in finding a path forward that reflects a broader set of interests.

From a leadership perspective, this moment highlights an important aspect of governance: the ability to bring different stakeholders to the table and move toward resolution. In a state as large and complex as California, that process is rarely simple. It requires persistence, communication, and a willingness to engage with competing viewpoints.

At the same time, the policy has sparked broader conversations about scalability. As discussions continue around the future of leadership in the United States, including the potential national trajectory of figures like Newsom, California's policies are often viewed through a wider lens. Observers ask how these approaches might translate at the federal level, where economic conditions vary significantly from region to region.

What works in California—a state with a large economy, a strong labor presence, and a high cost of living—may require adjustment in other parts of the country. That does not diminish the policy's intent or impact; it simply reinforces the importance of context in economic decision-making.

Another related development is the ongoing conversation around wages in other sectors, including healthcare. Proposals to increase pay for healthcare workers reflect a similar goal: ensuring that essential roles are compensated in a way that reflects their importance. At the same time, these proposals introduce additional considerations around funding, particularly in systems that rely on public programs and reimbursements.

Supporters of higher wages often point to research suggesting that increased income can reduce reliance on public assistance and strengthen local economies. When workers have more spending power, that money tends to circulate within communities, supporting businesses and generating economic activity. This perspective bȝcꝏ wages not just as a cost, but as an investment.

Others emphasize the importance of pacing and structure—ensuring that wage increases are implemented in a way that allows businesses and institutions to adapt effectively. These viewpoints are not mutually exclusive. In many ways, they reflect different aspects of the same goal: building an economy that is both fair and sustainable.

What becomes clear is that there is no single narrative that fully captures the impact of a policy like this. It is neither purely beneficial nor inherently problematic. It is a complex shift within a dynamic system, one that will continue to evolve over time.

For California, this moment represents another step in its ongoing role as a policy innovator. The state has often been at the forefront of economic and social change, testing ideas that later influence national conversations. That position comes with both opportunity and responsibility. It allows California to lead, but it also means that outcomes are closely watched.

For leaders, including Newsom, the challenge is to remain responsive. Policies do not end at implementation—they require monitoring, adjustment, and, when necessary, recalibration. The most effective leadership is not defined by avoiding complexity, but by engaging with it thoughtfully and consistently.

For workers, the impact is more immediate. A higher wage can mean greater stability, more options, and a stronger foundation for the future. For businesses, it means adapting within a changing environment— finding ways to remain competitive while meeting new standards. For consumers, it may mean adjustments in pricing, balanced against a broader shift in economic participation.

In the end, the question is not simply about the cost of higher wages. It is about the value they create, the systems they influence, and the direction they point toward. California's experience offers insight into all of these dimensions, providing a real-world example of how economic policy plays out beyond theory.

As the state continues to evolve, so too will the conversation. And within that conversation lies a larger truth: meaningful progress is rarely simple, but it is often worth pursuing when approached with clarity, balance, and a willingness to adapt.

Prison Policies and Public Safety

In a state as large and complex as California, few issues generate as much attention—or as much nuance—as public safety and criminal justice. Under the leadership of Gavin Newsom, these topics have remained at the center of ongoing policy evolution. His approach to prison reform, sentencing adjustments, and rehabilitation has sparked a wide range of reactions, reflecting the broader national conversation about how justice systems should function in the modern era.

At its core, the debate is not simply about being "tough" or "lenient" on crime. It is about how to balance accountability, public safety, rehabilitation, and long-term outcomes. These are not easy variables to align, particularly in a state with a prison system as large as California's.

When Newsom took office in 2019, California's prison population was already the subject of significant discussion. Years of policy changes, court rulings, and reform efforts had begun to reshape how the state approached incarceration. Concerns about overcrowding, costs, and the effectiveness of long-term imprisonment had prompted leaders across multiple administrations to explore alternatives.

During Newsom's tenure, that trend continued. The state moved toward reducing its prison population through a combination of sentencing reforms, expanded parole considerations, and adjustments made during the COVID-19 pandemic. As a result, the overall number of incarcerated individuals declined significantly over time. Supporters of these changes view them as part of a broader effort to create a more efficient and rehabilitative system—one that focuses not just on punishment, but on reducing repeat offenses over the long term.

At the same time, these shifts have prompted important conversations among law enforcement officials, policymakers, and community leaders. Individuals such as Chad Bianco have publicly expressed concerns about how these policies are implemented at the local level. From that perspective, the focus is on ensuring that communities remain safe and that any changes to the system are carefully managed.

These differing viewpoints highlight a key reality: criminal justice reform is not a single decision, but an ongoing process. Each adjustment—whether related to sentencing, parole, or prison capacity—creates downstream effects that must be monitored and addressed. The question is not whether reform should happen, but how it should be structured to achieve the best possible outcomes.

One visible component of Newsom's approach has been the decision to close certain state prison facilities. From a policy standpoint, this reflects a belief that a reduced prison population allows for consolidation of resources and a shift toward alternative strategies, including rehabilitation programs and community-based initiatives. It also acknowledges the high cost of maintaining large correctional systems, particularly when population levels decline.

However, facility closures also raise practical considerations. Communities that rely on correctional institutions for employment may feel economic impact, and law enforcement agencies often seek clarity on how population shifts affect local responsibilities. These are not contradictions—they are part of the broader equation that policymakers must navigate.

Another layer of the discussion involves early release programs and parole evaluations. These mechanisms are designed to assess individual cases, taking into account behavior, rehabilitation progress, and risk factors. When implemented effectively, they can provide pathways for reintegration while maintaining oversight. At the same time, they require consistent standards and transparency to ensure public confidence.

Public safety remains the central concern in all of these conversations. Residents want to feel secure in their communities, and that expectation shapes how policies are perceived. When incidents occur involving individuals who have been released or are part of reform programs, they often become focal points in the broader debate. These moments can influence public perception quickly, even as the overall system continues to evolve.

It is also important to recognize that crime trends are influenced by multiple factors—economic conditions, social dynamics, policing strategies, and community resources, among others. Isolating any single policy as the sole driver of outcomes can oversimplify a highly complex issue. What matters is how all of these elements interact and how leaders respond to emerging data over time.

The COVID-19 pandemic added another layer of complexity to the system. Like many states, California had to make rapid decisions to address health risks within correctional facilities. These decisions contributed to population reductions and accelerated certain policy discussions. In retrospect, the pandemic period has become a point of analysis for how emergency conditions intersect with long-term reform efforts.

From a leadership standpoint, moments like these require balancing urgency with caution. Decisions must be made quickly, but they also carry lasting implications. This is where adaptability becomes essential. Effective governance is not static—it evolves based on outcomes, feedback, and changing conditions.

As Newsom's national profile has grown, so too has interest in how his policies might translate beyond California. Conversations about potential future leadership roles naturally bring state-level decisions into a broader context. Observers look at California as a case study—not as a perfect model, but as a real-world example of how reform efforts play out in practice.

Scaling any policy to the national level introduces new variables. The United States is not a single economic or social environment; it is a collection of regions with distinct characteristics. What works in one state may require modification in another. This does not diminish the value of innovation—it simply reinforces the need for flexibility in application.

Within this framework, criminal justice reform remains one of the most closely watched areas. It touches on fundamental questions about fairness, safety, and the role of government. Leaders who engage with these issues are often navigating competing priorities, each with its own set of expectations.

Supporters of Newsom's approach often emphasize the long-term benefits of reducing incarceration rates, particularly when paired with rehabilitation and reentry programs. The goal is to address root causes and create pathways that reduce the likelihood of repeat offenses. From this perspective, reform is not about reducing accountability, but about improving outcomes.

Others highlight the importance of maintaining strong safeguards and ensuring that public safety remains the top priority. They advocate for careful implementation, clear communication, and ongoing evaluation of results. These perspectives are not mutually exclusive—they reflect different aspects of the same objective: building a system that works.

Public trust plays a critical role in this process. Confidence in leadership is shaped not only by policy decisions, but by how those decisions are communicated and adjusted over time. Transparency, consistency, and responsiveness all contribute to that trust. When people feel informed and included in the conversation, they are more likely to engage constructively with change.

California's experience underscores the importance of this balance. It shows that reform is not a one-time action, but a continuous effort that requires attention, data, and collaboration. It also demonstrates that leadership in this space involves navigating both immediate concerns and long-term goals.

As the national conversation around criminal justice continues, the lessons from California will remain relevant. They provide insight into what works, what needs refinement, and how different approaches can be integrated. More importantly, they highlight the reality that progress often comes with complexity.

For Newsom, the path forward—whether within California or on a larger stage—will likely continue to involve engaging with these issues in a visible and active way. For the public, the focus will remain on outcomes: safer communities, fair systems, and policies that reflect both accountability and opportunity.

In the end, the discussion around prison policies and public safety is not about choosing between reform and stability. It is about finding a way to achieve both. California's ongoing efforts offer a window into that process, providing a perspective that extends far beyond state lines and into the broader future of governance in the United States.

Retail Challenges and Economic Pressure

In major markets like San Francisco and Los Angeles, the retail landscape has been undergoing noticeable change. Storefronts that once symbolized growth and consumer confidence now reflect a more complex reality—one shaped by shifting economic conditions, evolving consumer behavior, and ongoing public safety concerns. Under the leadership of Gavin Newsom, these developments have become part of a broader conversation about how states respond to retail theft, economic pressure, and community stability.

Retail has always been sensitive to change. It sits at the intersection of supply chains, pricing, labor, and consumer confidence. When one element shifts, the effects are often felt quickly across the entire system. In recent years, retailers—both large national chains and small independent businesses—have had to adapt to a combination of inflation, changing shopping habits, and increased operational challenges.

Companies such as Target and Nordstrom have publicly discussed the financial impact of inventory loss, often referred to in the industry as "shrink." This term encompasses a range of factors, including theft, administrative errors, and supply chain discrepancies. While organized retail crime has received significant attention, industry experts note that shrink is a multifaceted issue that cannot be attributed to a single cause.

At the same time, there has been increased visibility around coordinated theft incidents, sometimes referred to as organized retail crime. These events, often captured on video and shared widely, have contributed to a perception that retail environments are becoming more challenging to manage. For employees on the ground, this can translate into heightened concerns about safety and job conditions. For business owners, it introduces additional costs related to security, staffing, and loss prevention.

It is important, however, to view these developments within a broader economic context. Inflation, supply chain disruptions, and shifts in consumer spending patterns have all played a role in reshaping the retail environment. As costs rise, both businesses and consumers feel the pressure. Retailers may adjust pricing or operations, while consumers may change purchasing habits or reduce discretionary spending. These interconnected dynamics make it difficult to isolate any single factor as the defining cause.

From a policy standpoint, California has been part of a larger national movement toward criminal justice reform. Changes to how certain offenses are categorized and prosecuted have sparked ongoing debate about their impact on public safety and economic activity. Supporters of these reforms emphasize the importance of focusing law enforcement resources on more serious crimes and reducing long-term incarceration for nonviolent offenses. They argue that this approach can lead to more efficient systems and better long-term outcomes.

At the same time, law enforcement officials and business leaders have raised concerns about how these policies are experienced at the local level. Individuals such as Chad Bianco have pointed to the need for clear accountability and consistent enforcement, particularly when it comes to repeat offenses or organized activity. These perspectives highlight the importance of implementation—how policies translate from legislation into day-to-day reality.

This is where the conversation becomes more nuanced. Public safety and economic vitality are closely linked. When businesses feel confident in their operating environment, they are more likely to invest, expand, and hire. When that confidence is challenged, even temporarily, it can lead to adjustments in strategy, including store closures, relocations, or changes in operating hours.

In cities like San Francisco, the closure of certain retail locations has drawn national attention. While these decisions are often influenced by multiple factors—leases, foot traffic, online competition, and overall strategy—public safety considerations have been part of the discussion. These moments tend to become symbolic, representing broader concerns about the direction of urban retail.

At the same time, it is important to recognize that retail is evolving across the country, not just in California. The rise of e-commerce, changing consumer expectations, and new business models have transformed how companies approach physical locations. Some closures reflect these long-term shifts as much as they reflect short-term challenges.

From a leadership perspective, addressing retail concerns requires coordination across multiple areas: law enforcement, economic policy, community engagement, and business development. It is not a single-policy issue—it is a systems issue. Effective responses often involve partnerships between government agencies, private sector leaders, and local communities.

Efforts to address retail theft have included increased collaboration between retailers and law enforcement, investments in technology, and targeted legislation aimed at organized crime networks. These approaches reflect an understanding that prevention, enforcement, and adaptation must work together.

Public perception also plays a significant role. Highly visible incidents can shape how people feel about safety, even if broader data presents a more complex picture. Managing that perception requires clear communication, transparency, and consistent action. When communities feel informed and engaged, confidence tends to follow.

As conversations continue around national leadership and future political direction, California's experience is often viewed as a reference point. Observers look at how challenges are identified, how policies are implemented, and how adjustments are made over time. This does not mean that one state's approach can be directly applied to the entire country, but it does provide insight into how large-scale systems respond to pressure.

If leaders from state-level roles move onto the national stage, they bring with them both experience and perspective. The key question is how that experience translates across different regions, each with its own economic structure and community dynamics. Flexibility becomes essential—what works in one environment may require refinement in another.

For retailers, the path forward involves continued adaptation. Many are investing in new technologies, rethinking store layouts, and strengthening partnerships with local communities. These strategies are not just reactive—they are part of a broader effort to build resilience in a changing market.

For policymakers, the focus remains on balance. Supporting businesses while addressing social and economic challenges requires an approach that is both proactive and responsive. It means recognizing that economic health and public safety are interconnected, and that progress in one area supports stability in the other.

For communities, the goal is straightforward: safe, accessible, and vibrant places to live, work, and shop. Achieving that goal requires collaboration at every level—government, business, and individual participation.

In the end, the conversation around retail challenges is not about assigning blame—it is about understanding complexity. It is about recognizing that economic systems are dynamic, and that meaningful solutions require a combination of policy, innovation, and engagement.

California's experience offers a window into that process. It shows that challenges can coexist with opportunity, and that periods of adjustment often lead to new approaches and stronger systems over time. As the landscape continues to evolve, the focus will remain on building environments where businesses can thrive, communities can feel secure, and economic participation remains accessible to all.

That balance—between growth and stability, between innovation and accountability—is what ultimately defines long-term success, not just for one state, but for any economy navigating change at scale.

Fiscal Shifts and National Considerations

Few issues define leadership more clearly than fiscal management. Budgets are not just numbers on a page—they are reflections of priorities, assumptions, and expectations about the future. In California, under Gavin Newsom, the state's financial position has moved through a significant cycle in a relatively short period of time, sparking broader discussion about revenue volatility, spending commitments, and long-term sustainability.

Just a few years ago, California found itself in a remarkably strong fiscal position. During the post-pandemic economic rebound, the state experienced a surge in tax revenues, driven in part by capital gains, high-income earners, and a strong performance in sectors like technology and finance. This led to what was widely described as a substantial budget surplus —one of the largest in the state's history.

At the time, this surplus was seen by many as a sign of economic resilience. It created opportunities for expanded investment in areas such as education, healthcare, and direct relief efforts for residents. Policymakers, including Newsom, viewed it as a chance to address longstanding challenges while supporting recovery from the economic disruption caused by the pandemic.

However, as with many revenue surges tied to specific economic conditions, the strength of that moment proved to be temporary. California's tax structure is heavily influenced by high-income earners, particularly through capital gains tied to the stock market. While this can generate significant revenue during periods of growth, it also introduces a high degree of variability when markets shift.

As economic conditions began to normalize and certain sectors cooled, state revenues declined more sharply than initially anticipated. The result was a projected budget deficit that required adjustments in spending, planning, and expectations. This shift did not occur in isolation—it reflected broader economic trends, including inflation, changes in investment activity, and evolving consumer behavior.

What California's experience illustrates is not simply a rise and fall in numbers, but the challenge of managing a revenue system that is both highly productive and inherently unpredictable. During periods of expansion, it can create opportunities for bold initiatives. During periods of contraction, it requires careful recalibration.

From a policy perspective, the decisions made during surplus periods are often where long-term impact is determined. Investments in social programs, infrastructure, and public services can provide meaningful benefits, but they also create ongoing commitments. The key question becomes how those commitments are sustained when revenue levels change.

In California's case, the transition from surplus to deficit has led to a renewed focus on budgeting discipline, prioritization, and the role of reserve funds. Like many states, California maintains a "rainy-day" reserve designed to help stabilize finances during downturns. The effectiveness of such reserves depends not only on their size, but on how they are integrated into broader fiscal strategy.

These dynamics are not unique to California. They are part of a larger conversation about how governments at all levels manage economic cycles. The balance between investing in growth and maintaining fiscal flexibility is a constant challenge, particularly in environments where revenue streams are closely tied to market performance.

As discussions continue around national leadership and future political direction, California's fiscal experience often enters the conversation as a point of reference. Observers consider how a leader's approach to budgeting, forecasting, and spending might translate to the federal level, where the scale is significantly larger and the variables more complex.

Under Joe Biden, the federal government has also navigated a period of economic transition. Pandemic-related spending, inflationary pressures, and shifts in monetary policy have all contributed to an evolving fiscal landscape. These conditions underscore the importance of adaptability in economic governance.

If leaders with state-level experience move into national roles, they bring with them both lessons and perspectives shaped by those experiences. The key consideration is how those lessons are applied. State budgets and federal budgets operate under different constraints and structures, but the underlying principles—accurate forecasting, disciplined spending, and long-term planning—remain consistent.

One of the most important takeaways from California's recent fiscal shifts is the need for realistic revenue projections. Overly optimistic assumptions can create challenges when conditions change, while overly conservative estimates may limit opportunities for investment. Finding the right balance requires both data and judgment.

Another critical factor is spending structure. One-time surpluses are often best aligned with one-time investments, while ongoing programs benefit from stable, predictable funding sources. Aligning these elements effectively helps reduce the risk of future imbalances.

Transparency also plays a central role. Clear communication about fiscal conditions, assumptions, and adjustments builds public trust and allows for more informed decision-making. In complex systems, understanding the "why" behind financial decisions is just as important as the decisions themselves.

At the same time, it is important to recognize that fiscal policy does not operate in a vacuum. It is closely connected to broader economic conditions, including employment, business activity, and global markets. External factors can influence outcomes in ways that are not always predictable, reinforcing the need for flexibility and contingency planning.

For California, the current fiscal environment represents a period of adjustment rather than a fixed outcome. Budgets evolve, priorities shift, and new strategies emerge in response to changing conditions. This is the nature of economic governance—dynamic, responsive, and continuously refined.

For the nation, the conversation is similar but amplified. Federal decisions influence not just one state, but an entire network of economies, industries, and communities. The stakes are higher, but the principles remain the same: balance, discipline, and adaptability.

Supporters of Newsom's approach often highlight the importance of using periods of economic strength to invest in people and infrastructure. They argue that these investments can create long-term value, even if short-term adjustments are required. From this perspective, fiscal policy is not just about maintaining balance sheets, but about shaping future outcomes.

Others emphasize the importance of caution, particularly when dealing with variable revenue sources. They advocate for building stronger buffers, pacing new commitments, and ensuring that spending aligns with sustainable funding levels. These viewpoints reflect a focus on stability and risk management.

In reality, effective fiscal leadership often incorporates elements of both perspectives. It requires the ability to invest when conditions allow, while also preparing for periods of uncertainty. It is less about choosing one approach over the other, and more about integrating them in a way that supports long-term stability.

As California continues to navigate its fiscal path, the lessons emerging from this period will remain relevant. They offer insight into how large, complex economies respond to change and how leadership decisions shape those responses.

Ultimately, the conversation is not about labeling outcomes as success or failure. It is about understanding the factors that drive those outcomes and applying that understanding to future decisions. In a world where economic conditions can shift quickly, that level of awareness becomes one of the most valuable tools any leader can have.

And as the national conversation continues to evolve, those lessons—grounded in real-world experience—

will play an important role in shaping what comes next.

A National Profile in the Making

As Gavin Newsom continues to operate on one of the most visible political stages in the country, his role has increasingly drawn attention beyond California. In modern politics, the line between state leadership and national influence is often fluid. Governors of large, high-impact states frequently find themselves shaping conversations that extend far beyond their borders, and Newsom is no exception.

In recent years, his public appearances, messaging, and policy framing have reflected a broader engagement with national issues. His State of the State address, delivered through a prerecorded format and distributed across digital platforms, offered a clear example of this shift in communication style. Rather than a traditional legislative address focused solely on state operations, the speech incorporated themes that resonated on a wider stage—democracy, national identity, and the direction of the country as a whole.

Newsom's references to historical leadership, including figures like Culbert Olson, were used to frame present-day challenges within a larger narrative. By drawing parallels between past and present, he positioned California as part of an ongoing national story—one that involves defining values and responding to periods of uncertainty. This type of messaging is not unusual for leaders with growing national visibility. It reflects an effort to connect local governance with broader themes that resonate across state lines.

At the same time, communication strategies like this can generate different reactions depending on the audience. For some, the emphasis on national issues signals leadership that is engaged, forward-thinking, and willing to participate in larger conversations. For others, it raises questions about focus—particularly in a state where residents continue to navigate challenges related to housing, affordability, and cost of living.

Public opinion data has reflected this complexity. Surveys conducted by organizations such as the Public Policy Institute of California have shown a range of perspectives on the state's direction and leadership performance. These variations are not unusual in a state as large and diverse as California, where regional priorities and economic conditions can differ significantly. What they do highlight, however, is the importance of maintaining a strong connection between statewide leadership and local concerns.

Newsom's increasing presence in national discussions has also been evident through his participation in high-profile events and debates. His televised exchange with Ron DeSantis, for example, placed him directly in a national policy conversation, contrasting different approaches to governance and highlighting the ideological differences between states. These moments serve multiple purposes—they inform, they persuade, and they position.

From a strategic standpoint, this level of visibility can be seen as part of a broader political trajectory. Leaders who demonstrate the ability to communicate effectively on national issues often become part of future leadership discussions. This does not necessarily indicate a specific timeline or intention, but it does place them within a wider field of consideration.

At the same time, the responsibilities of governing a state like California remain substantial. With one of the largest economies in the world and a population that spans a wide range of industries and communities, the role demands consistent attention to detail and responsiveness to evolving challenges. Issues such as housing availability, public safety, infrastructure, and economic opportunity require ongoing focus and coordination.

Balancing these responsibilities with a growing national profile is not a new challenge in American politics. Many leaders have navigated similar paths, using their state-level experience as a platform for broader engagement while continuing to manage the day-to-day realities of governance. The effectiveness of that balance often becomes a defining factor in how their leadership is perceived.

Newsom's personal and logistical decisions, including maintaining ties to multiple regions within California, reflect the realities of leading in a state where both the capital and other regions play important roles. California's geographic and economic diversity means that leadership is not confined to a single location—it requires presence and awareness across multiple areas.

Timing and messaging also play a role in shaping perception. The scheduling of major addresses, policy announcements, and public appearances often intersects with broader national events. Whether intentional or coincidental, these overlaps can influence how actions are interpreted. In a media environment that operates around the clock, context becomes just as important as content.

Newsom's engagement with national topics—ranging from economic policy to social issues—has positioned him as a voice within the Democratic Party's broader conversation. His support for Joe Biden and his willingness to address contrasting viewpoints publicly have contributed to that role. For supporters, this represents active leadership and a commitment to shaping the party's direction. For others, it reinforces the importance of ensuring that state-level priorities remain front and center.

This dynamic reflects a larger question that applies to many leaders: how to effectively operate on multiple levels at once. State leadership requires precision and execution, while national engagement often involves broader messaging and vision. The ability to integrate both is what defines long-term effectiveness.

For residents of California, the expectations are clear. They are looking for leadership that addresses immediate concerns while also positioning the state for future success. These goals are not mutually exclusive, but they do require careful alignment. When that alignment is strong, leadership feels cohesive. When it is less clear, questions naturally arise.

From a national perspective, figures like Newsom are often evaluated based on both their ideas and their track record. Observers look at how policies are implemented, how challenges are addressed, and how communication evolves over time. These factors contribute to a broader understanding of leadership style and capability.

It is also worth noting that ambition, in itself, is not inherently negative. In many cases, it drives innovation, encourages engagement, and expands the scope of what is possible. The key consideration is how that ambition is balanced with responsibility. Effective leadership requires both vision and execution—one without the other is rarely sufficient.

As conversations about the future of American leadership continue, Newsom's role will likely remain part of that dialogue. His experience in California provides a foundation, while his national engagement expands his reach. The intersection of those two elements is where much of the discussion takes place.

Ultimately, the question is not whether a leader can think beyond their current role—it is whether they can do so while maintaining strong performance within it. For Newsom, as for any leader in a similar position, that balance will continue to shape both perception and opportunity.

California, with all of its complexity and influence, remains central to that equation. It is both a proving ground and a platform—one that offers lessons, challenges, and opportunities in equal measure. How those elements come together will determine not only the trajectory of one leader, but also the broader conversation about leadership in the years ahead.

www.ingramcontent.com/pod-product-compliance
Lightning Source LLC
Chambersburg PA
CBHW051648250726
48653CB00007B/2554